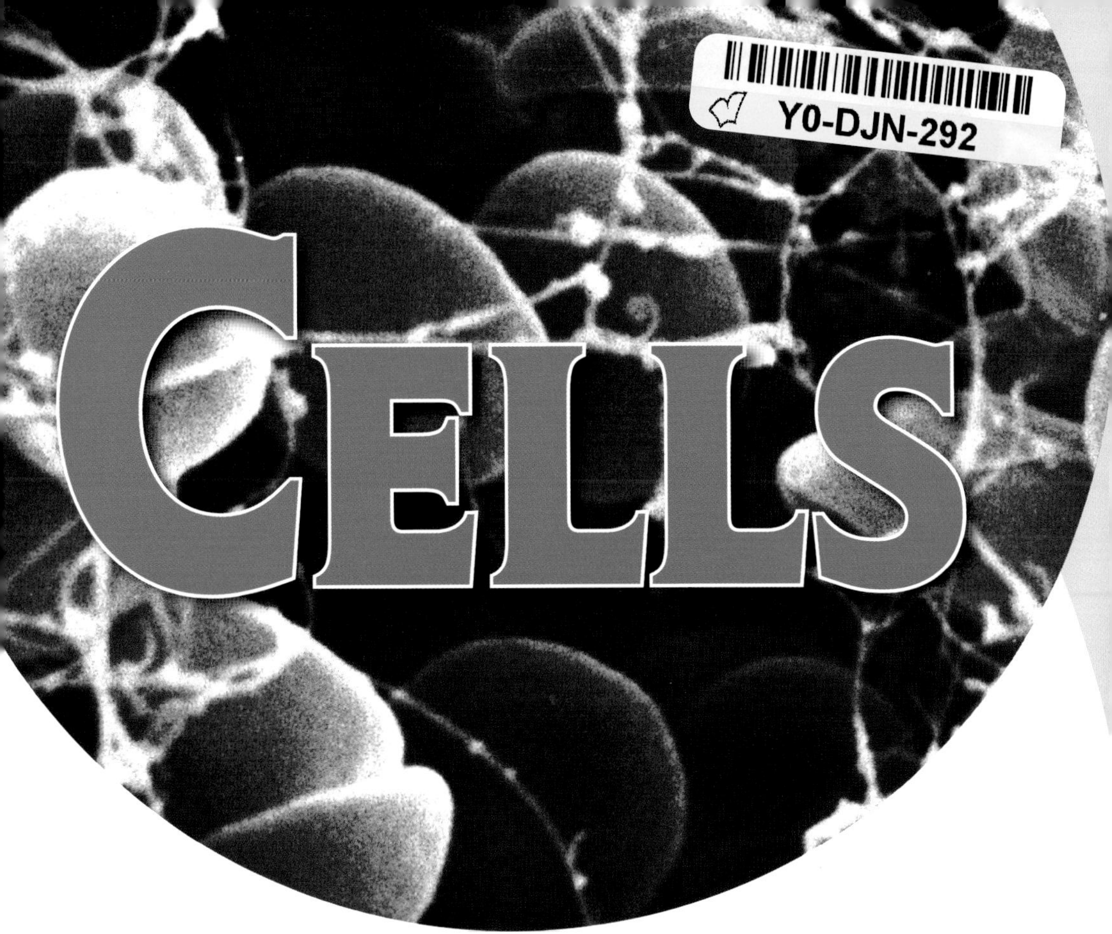

Cells

by Kathy French

Table of Contents

Introduction

Believe it or not, elephants, butterflies, sunflowers, and you all have something in common. Can you guess what it is? **Cells**! Elephants, butterflies, sunflowers, and you are all living things. And all living things are made of cells.

Some living things are made of only one cell. But an adult human is made up of trillions of cells! Not all human cells are the same. There are brain cells, nerve cells, muscle cells, and others.

Each type of human cell has a different purpose and helps us do a different task. If it weren't for cells, you wouldn't be able to work, play, or eat. Actually, if it weren't for cells, you would not *be* you at all!

Read this book to learn more about cells. Find out how cells were first discovered and who discovered them. Learn about the different parts of a cell, and what each part does. Find out how plant cells and human cells are alike and how they are different. Meet "good" cells, "bad" cells, and cell invaders.

Cells: An Accidental Discovery

If every living thing is made up of cells, you might wonder why you can't see them. The answer is that most cells are microscopic. That means they are so small that they can't be seen without a microscope. So how did scientists find cells? It was by accident! The first person to see cells wasn't even looking for them.

Robert Hooke was the first person to discover and describe cells. In 1665, he looked at the bark of a cork tree with a handmade microscope. He saw tiny compartments that made up the bark. Hooke chose the word *cell* to describe what he saw. Why? Because he thought what he saw looked like tiny rooms, or cells.

This illustration of cork cells represents Hooke's first look at plant cells.

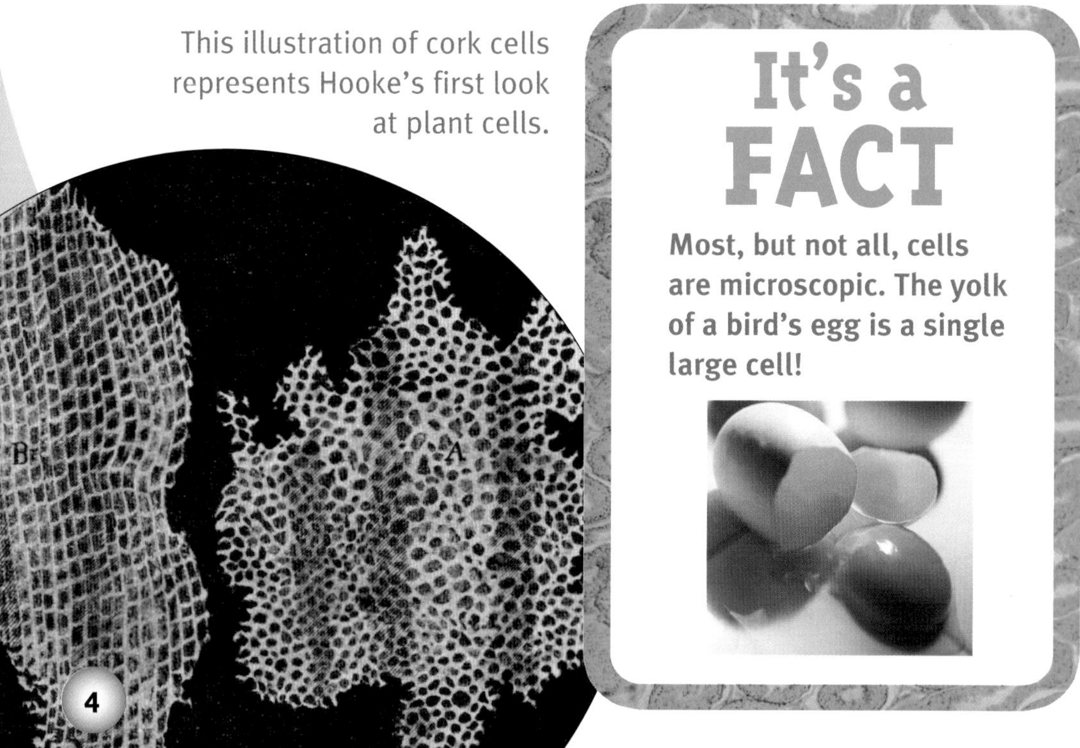

It's a FACT

Most, but not all, cells are microscopic. The yolk of a bird's egg is a single large cell!

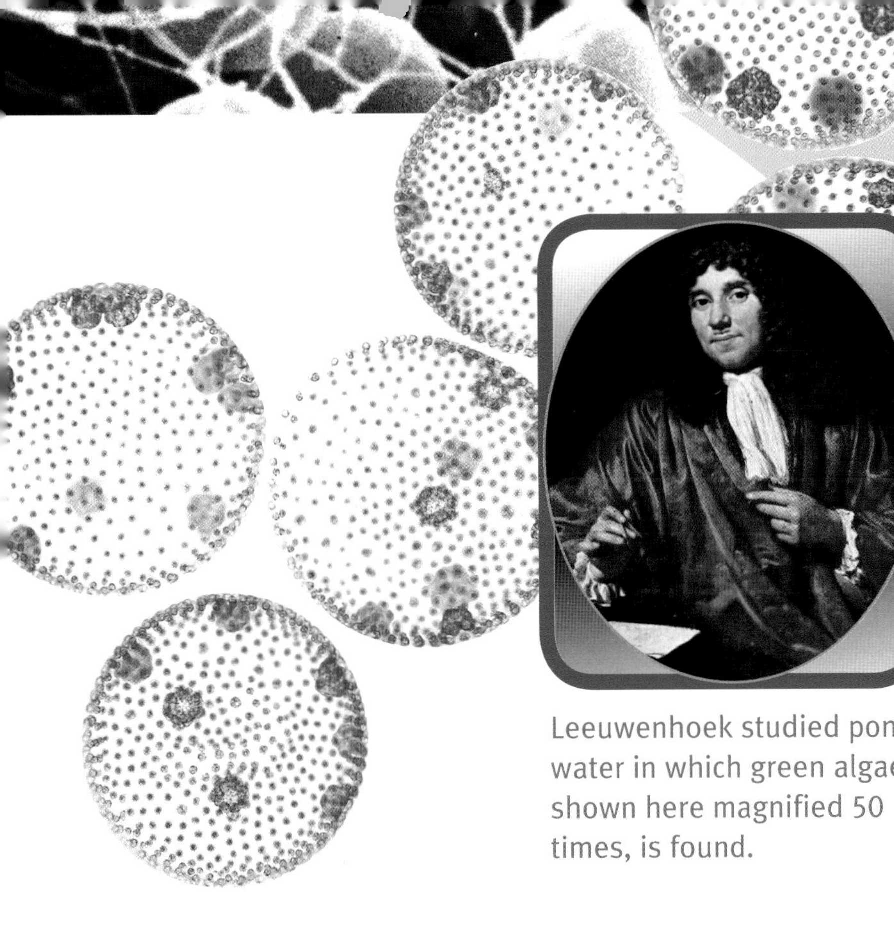

Leeuwenhoek studied pond water in which green algae, shown here magnified 50 times, is found.

Anton van Leeuwenhoek (LAY-ven-huk) worked as a cloth merchant in the Netherlands, a country in Europe. He made his own microscopes. At about the same time that Hooke saw cork cells, Leeuwenhoek studied pond water. What he was able to see with one of his microscopes was amazing! He saw tiny creatures swimming around in a drop of water. He called these one-celled creatures animalcules (a-nih-MAL-kyoolz), which means "little animals."

Leeuwenhoek used his microscope to look at blood. He was also the first person to see **bacteria** under the microscope. Bacteria are one-celled living things that can cause disease in people, plants, or animals. These discoveries made Leeuwenhoek famous all over the world.

Scientists had been using microscopes to look at cells since 1665. But no one knew for sure that all living things were made up of cells until the late 1830s. In 1838, a German botanist (a scientist who studies plants) by the name of Matthias Schleiden (SHLIGH-dihn) figured out that all plants are made of cells. Another German scientist, Theodor Schwann, concluded that all animals are also made of cells.

Then in 1858, Rudolf Virchow (FIHR-koh), a German doctor, realized that all diseases were diseases of the cell. He believed that in order to understand a disease, a doctor had to understand how it affected cells.

Scientists were able to make those discoveries because of improvements to microscopes.

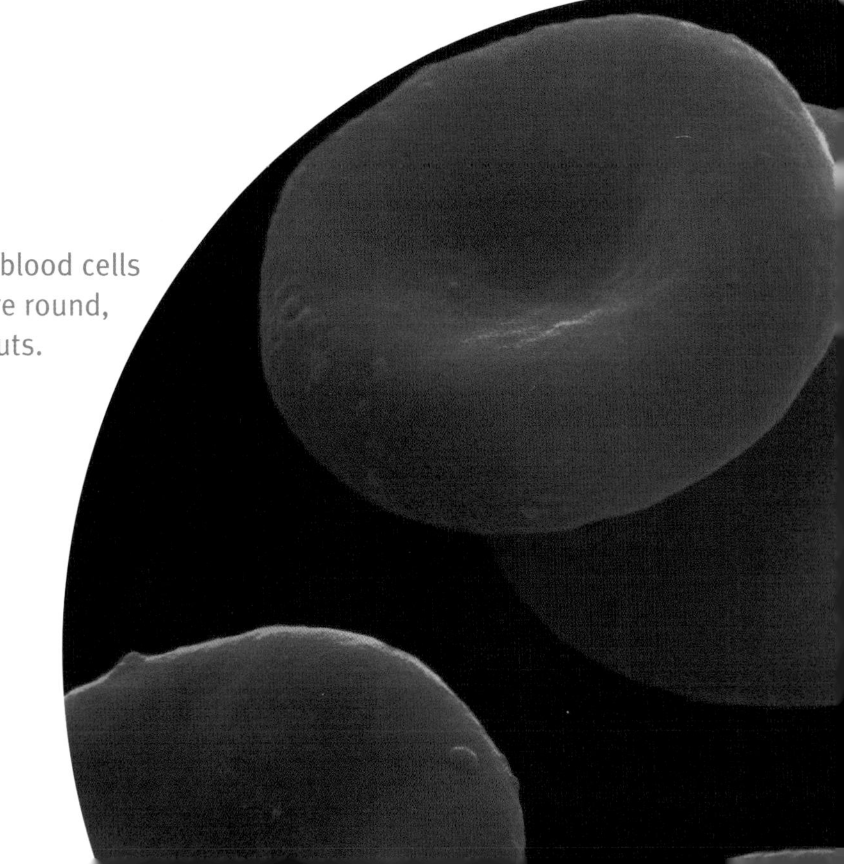

Healthy red blood cells like these are round, like doughnuts.

As microscopes with more lenses and stronger lenses were invented, scientists could see cells in much greater detail. Scientists learned that cells were made up of several parts and that each part had a different purpose.

Sickle cell anemia is a disease of the red blood cells. Instead of being round, the diseased cells become longer and crescent-shaped. They also have less hemoglobin (HEE-muh-gloh-bin), which gives blood its color.

History of the

Improvements in microscopes led to increased knowledge about cells.

1590

Dutch eyeglass maker Zacharias Janssen (YAHN-suhn) made the first microscope. It was a simple tube with a lens at each end.

1670

Robert Hooke improved the Janssen microscope by adding a stand with an oil lamp on it. The lamp could light up the object under the microscope.

1670s

Anton van Leeuwenhoek built a microscope that used one tiny lens. It magnified objects to almost 300 times their actual size and allowed him to see single-celled organisms.

Microscope

Late 1800s

A microscope similar to those used in schools today was invented. These microscopes are called "compound light microscopes." They can magnify objects up to 1,000 times their actual size.

Late 1800s

The first electron microscope was invented. An electron microscope sends a beam of tiny particles through thin slices of a sample. This microscope can magnify a sample up to 500,000 (half a million) times its actual size.

1981

The Scanning Tunneling Microscope, a type of electron microscope, was invented. It is used to see structures on the surface of a cell. It can create an image on a TV screen that is up to 100 million times as large as the sample.

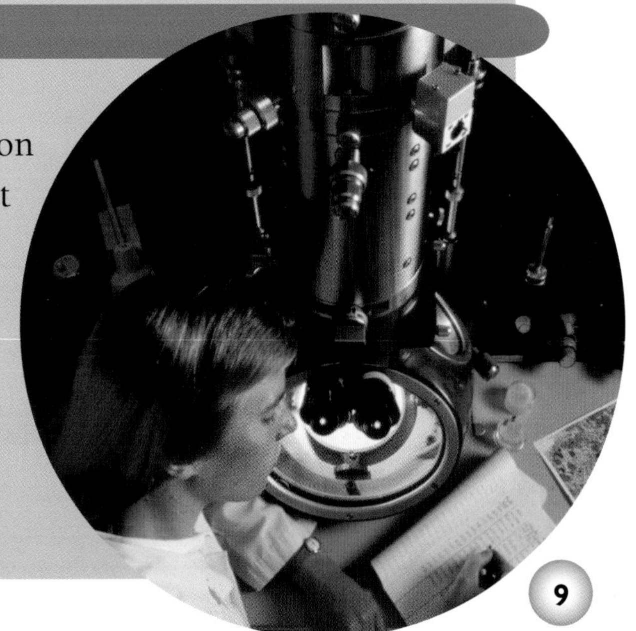

Activity

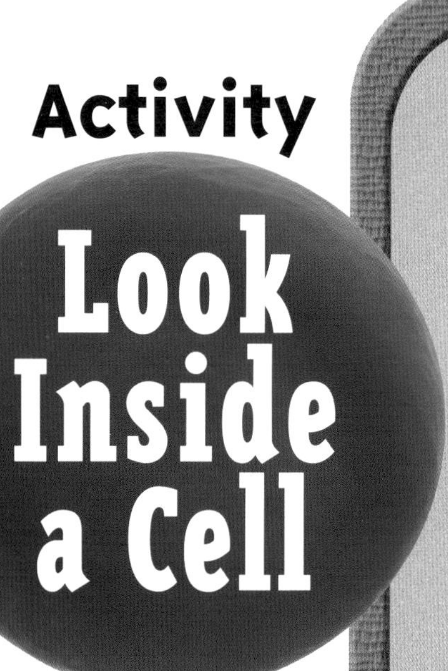

Look Inside a Cell

What You'll Need

- elodea (ih-LOH-dee-uh) plant (available in stores that sell aquarium supplies)
- water
- eyedropper
- tweezers
- microscope
- microscope slide
- cover slip for slide
- paper and pencil

What to Do

1. Use an eyedropper to add a drop of water to a microscope slide.
2. Use tweezers to tear off a small, thin elodea leaf.
3. Place the elodea leaf in the drop of water on the microscope slide.
4. Carefully place a cover slip on top of the water drop and elodea leaf.
5. Place the slide on a microscope and look for the elodea leaf cells under the lowest power of the microscope.
6. Focus the microscope. Then move to high power to see the elodea leaf cells up close.
7. Draw a picture of what you see.

Talk About It

1. Describe the shape of the elodea cells.
2. The shape of a cell has to do with its needs or the job it does. For example, your nerve cells are long and have many branches. The branches send messages throughout the body. Do you think cells from your body would look like elodea cells? Why or why not?

Cells in Action

The human body has about 200 kinds of cells. Each kind looks different from the others and does a different thing. But no matter their shape or size, all human cells have these same three main parts: a **cell membrane**, a **cytoplasm** (SY-tuh-pla-zum), and a **nucleus** (NOO-klee-us).

The cell membrane is like a skin. It forms the outside edge that separates the cell from everything around it. The cell membrane controls what materials go into and out of a cell. Everything a cell needs enters through the cell membrane. Harmful waste products leave the cell through the cell membrane.

The cytoplasm is a clear, thick, jelly-like substance inside the cell membrane. It supports other cell parts.

The cytoplasm contains **organelles**, or "little organs." Organelles do different things. For example, some organelles digest substances brought into the cell. Others help break down harmful substances, such as alcohol.

Cytoplasm is made of about 80 percent water and it is constantly moving. The movement of the cytoplasm allows substances to move from one place to another in the cell. It allows important nutrients, such as food and oxygen, to move through the cell. Cytoplasm also allows waste products to move to the outside of the cell.

Within the cytoplasm is the nucleus. The nucleus contains the cell's control center, which directs all the activities in the cell.

A Typical Human Cell

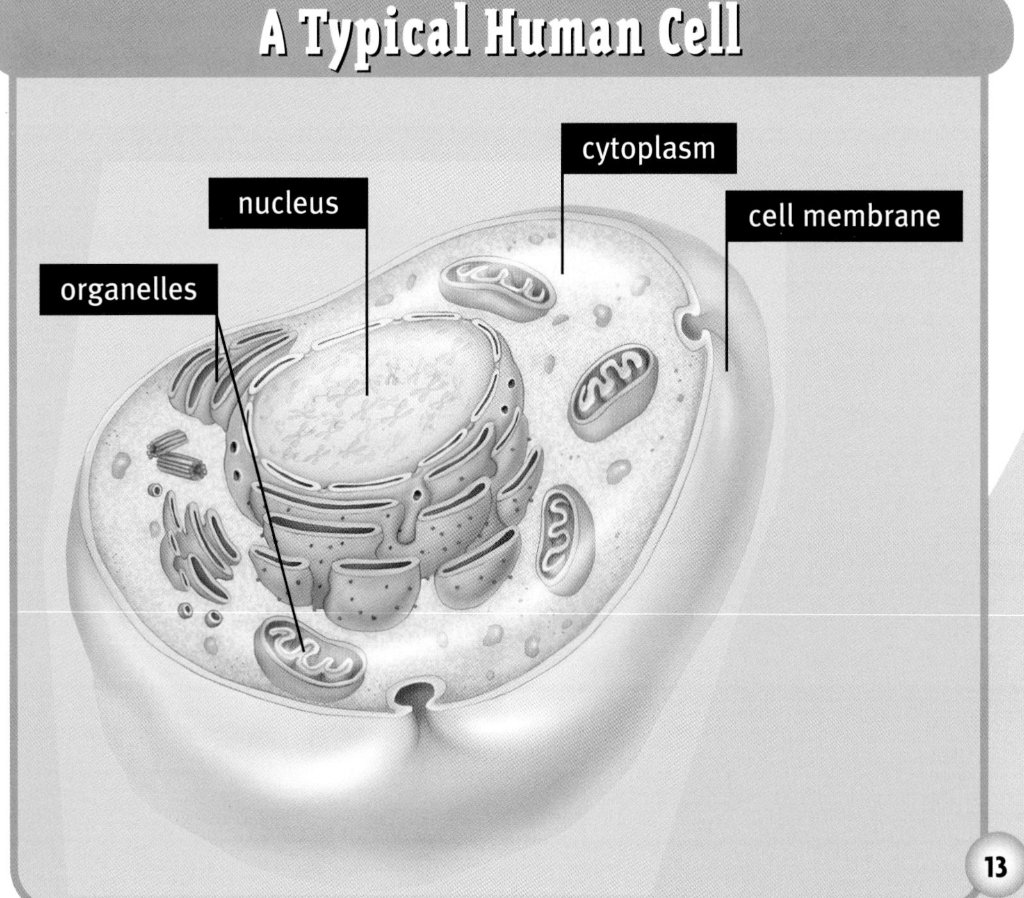

Within the nucleus are **chromosomes**. Chromosomes are long, coiled molecules made of DNA. DNA makes up **genes**. Genes have the instructions for building different types of cells. So, the segment of DNA within each gene is like a recipe or a secret code. The DNA contains all the information that a cell needs to create new cells.

It's a FACT

Scientists have combined the DNA from a goat with the DNA from a spider. The goat produces spider web cells in its milk. Fiber that is dried and spun from the goat's milk is five times stronger than steel. It can be used to make ropes, nets, fishing lines, and medical sutures—the thread doctors use for stitches.

A Cell Nucleus

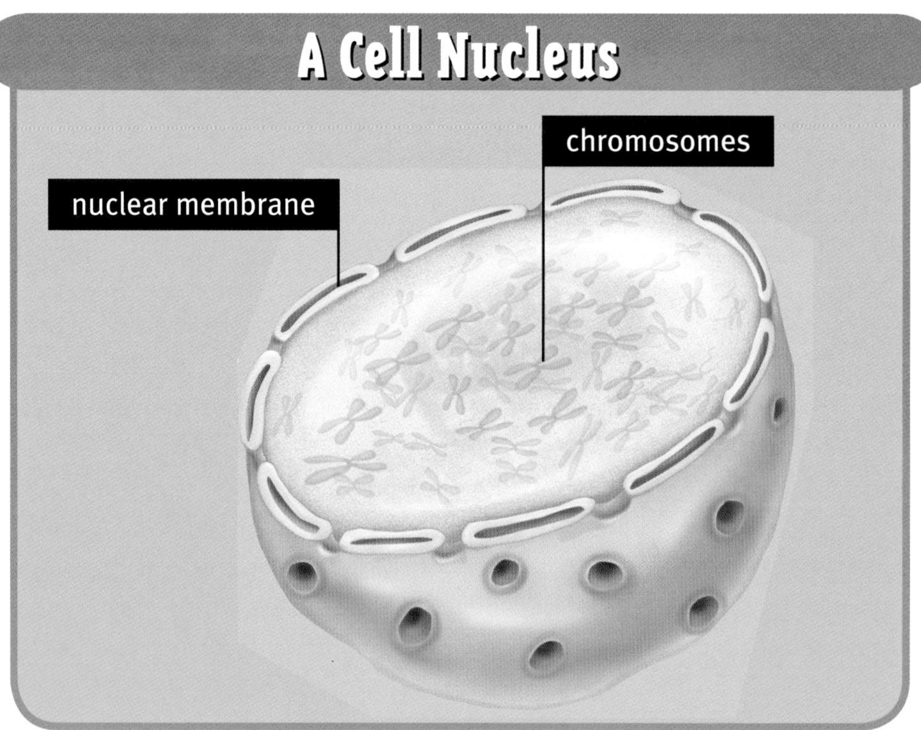

A DNA strand, or thread, looks like a twisted ladder. Scientists call the shape a "double helix" (HEE-liks). Each rung of the DNA ladder is made up of different chemicals. The DNA ladder may contain up to thousands of rungs. The chemicals on all these rungs can be arranged in many different orders. That's why all the living things on Earth look so different from one another. Unless you have an identical twin, no one has the same DNA that you have!

Identical twins have the same DNA.

a model of a DNA strand

They made a difference

In 1952, scientist Rosalind Franklin took an x-ray photograph of a DNA molecule. When scientists James Watson and Francis Crick saw the photograph in 1953, they created a DNA model. It showed that a DNA molecule looks like a twisted ladder. In 1962, Watson and Crick won the Nobel Prize for their work.

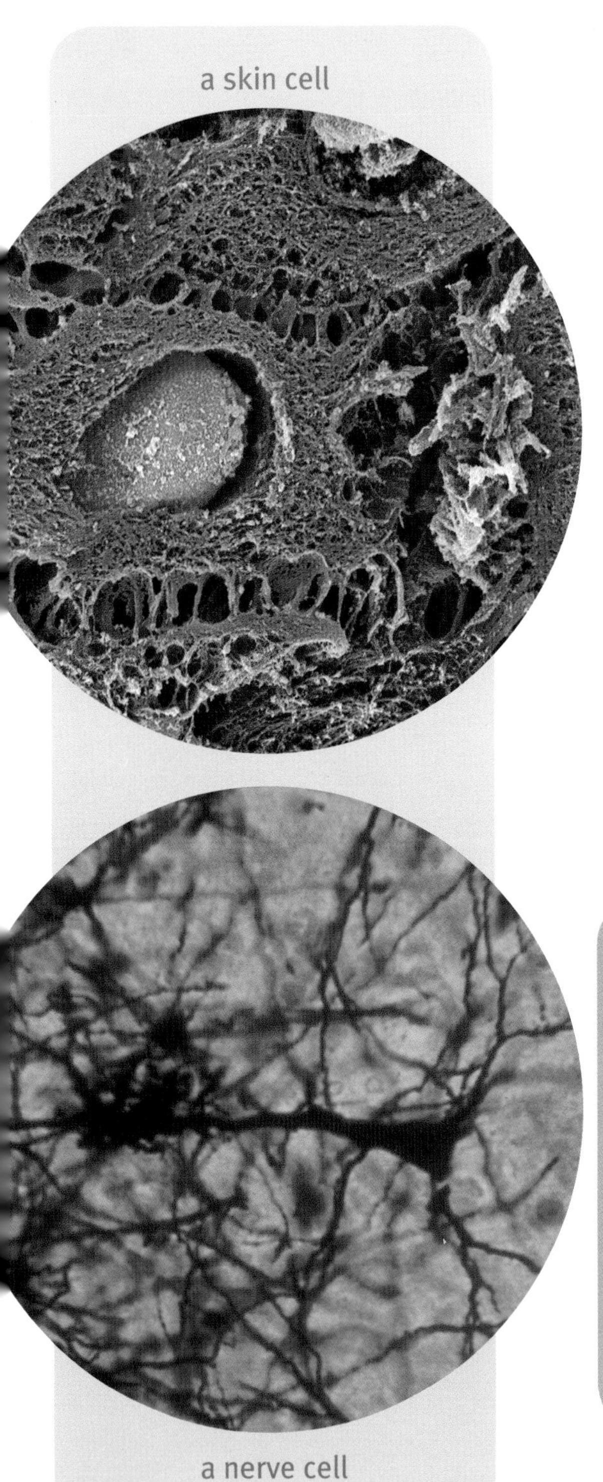

a skin cell

a nerve cell

DNA contains information on how to make all of the body's proteins. Proteins act as chemical messengers to help build different types of cells. For example, skin cells, muscle cells, and nerve cells are all made of specific combinations of proteins. The human body contains about 50,000 different kinds of proteins. These proteins are responsible for the color of our eyes, how tall we will grow, and whether our hair is straight or curly.

Careers in Science

Forensic scientists, or criminalists, are people who use scientific methods for solving crimes. One method of investigating a crime is called DNA fingerprinting. In DNA fingerprinting, forensic scientists obtain and analyze DNA from the cells of people suspected of being involved in a crime.

Animal cells and plant cells contain DNA, also. The DNA of plant cells contains different proteins than the DNA of animal cells. That's why plant cells have different structures than animal cells.

Plant cells have a hard **cell wall** outside of the cell membrane. The cell wall adds strength and support to the cell membrane. In woody plants, the cell walls are very sturdy. This is why trees can grow so strong and tall. Although the cell wall is stiff, materials such as food and water can pass through it easily.

A Plant Cell

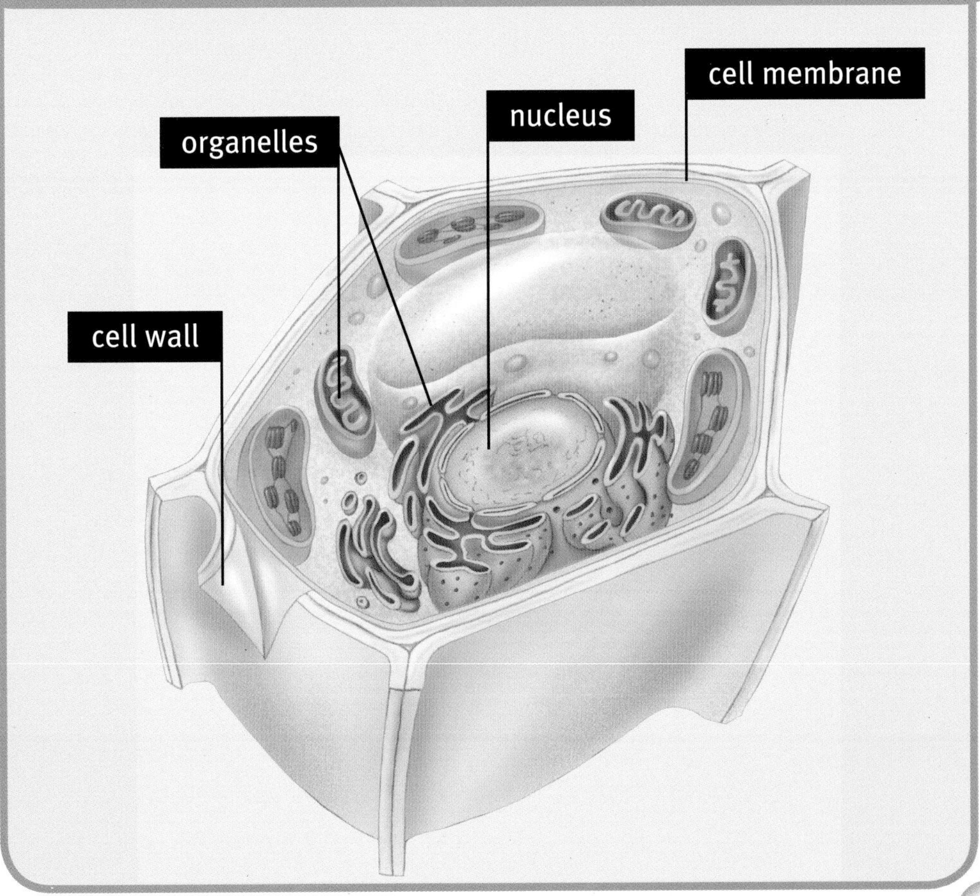

There's another difference between animal and plant cells. Plant cells can make their own food. They contain structures called **chloroplasts** (KLOR-uh-plasts), which are responsible for a process called **photosynthesis** (foh-toh-SIN-theh-sis).

Photosynthesis is the process by which green plants make their own food.

Everyday Science

The guar (GWAHR) plant produces a substance called a "gum" that helps make its cell walls stronger. This guar gum is used in ice cream to make it creamy and in shampoos and toothpastes to make them thicker.

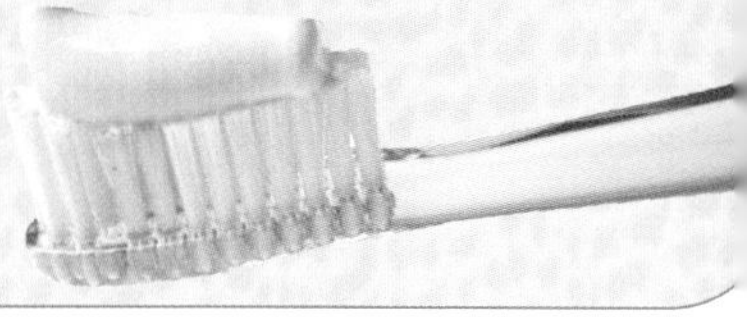

Photosynthesis Process

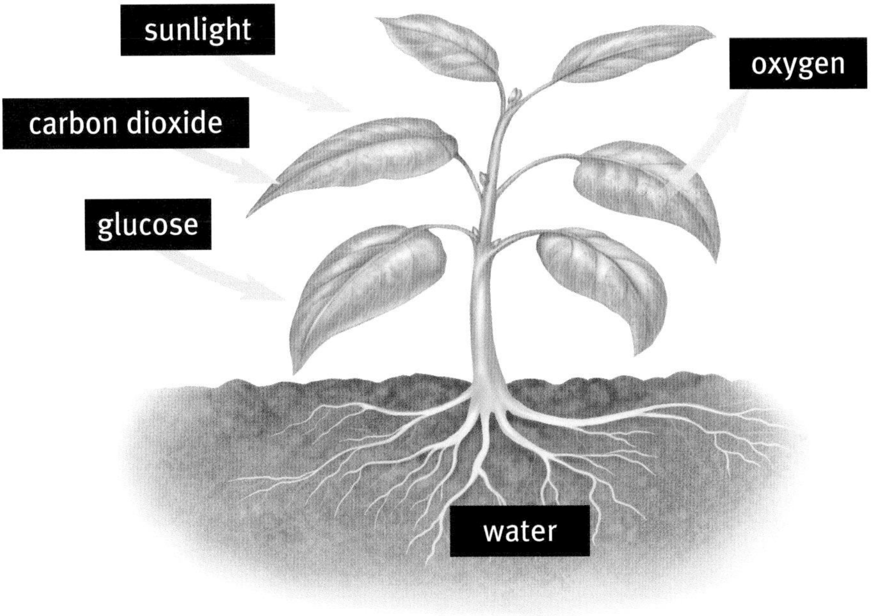

sunlight

carbon dioxide

glucose

oxygen

water

During photosynthesis, a chemical in the chloroplasts, called chlorophyll, uses energy from sunlight to combine water and carbon dioxide into glucose and oxygen. Glucose is a simple sugar that the plant uses for food. The plant stores the glucose in its stems or roots and releases the oxygen into the air.

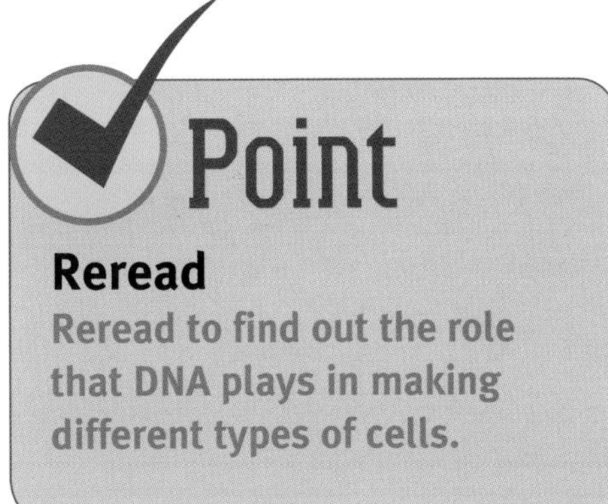

Good Cells, Bad Cells

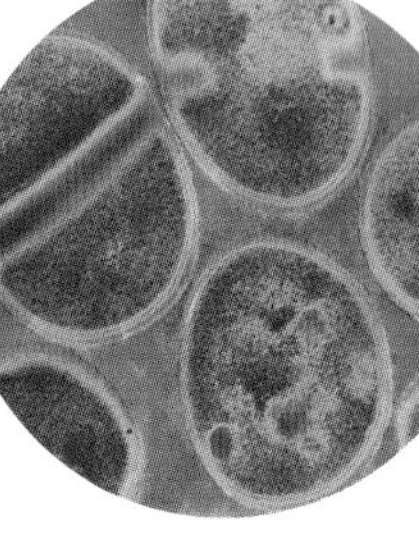
round bacteria

Bacteria

Bacteria are examples of single-celled organisms. There are three general shapes of bacteria: round, rod, and spiral.

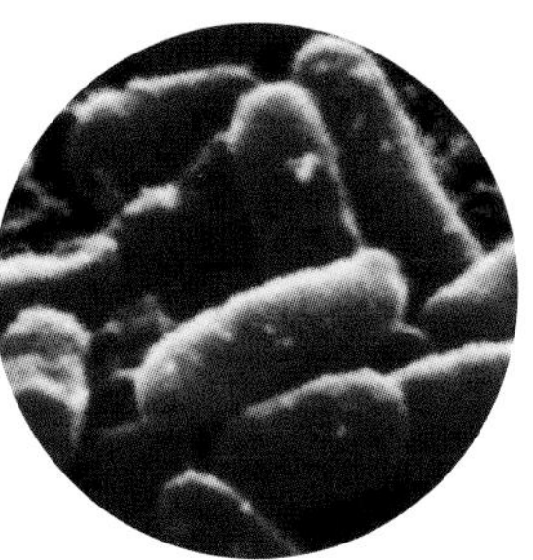
rod-shaped bacteria

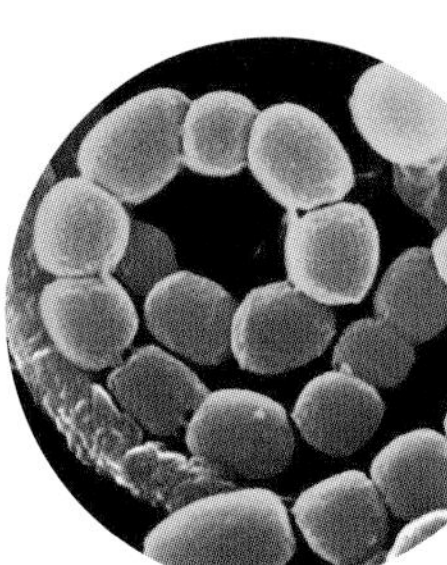
spiral bacteria

Some bacteria are harmful to humans. Have you ever had strep throat or an ear infection? If so, your body was invaded by bacteria! Bacteria love the inside of a human body. It is warm and moist—an excellent place for bacteria to grow.

Most of the time, your white blood cells are able to kill harmful bacteria in your body. But sometimes there are too many bacteria to kill. You might have to take antibiotics to kill those stubborn bacteria. Antibiotics are drugs that kill or weaken bacteria that cause disease.

It's a FACT

Bacteria can become resistant to an antibiotic. That means that the antibiotic can no longer kill the bacteria. One way that bacteria become resistant is by changing their cell membranes so that the antibiotic can't get through them. Scientists keep working to develop new antibiotics to fight bacteria.

Have you ever had food poisoning? Some foods, like milk, need to be refrigerated. If they are left at room temperature for too long, harmful bacteria grow in them. And some foods, like meat, need to be cooked at high temperatures to kill the bacteria in them. If we eat food that has not been properly stored, handled, or cooked, we end up with food poisoning.

Louis Pasteur (pas-TER)

They made a difference

In 1864, Louis Pasteur discovered that bacteria in milk were making people sick. Pasteur found that heating the milk before it was bottled would kill the bacteria. This process became known as pasteurization.

Lactobacillus acidophilus (lak-toh-buh-SIHL-ihs as-ih-DAH-fih-lihs)

Lactobacillus acidophilus is one bacteria used in foods like cheese and pickles to give them their tart taste.

Not all bacteria are harmful to humans. Many foods are produced with the help of bacteria. Bacteria in foods like cheeses, yogurt, pickles, vinegar, buttermilk, and sauerkraut give these foods their tart flavors. They also protect the foods from spoiling quickly.

Believe it or not, some bacteria actually help keep you healthy! Bacteria that live in your intestines help you to digest your food. Bacteria can also make vitamins that your body cannot make on its own.

Everyday Science

Yogurt contains lots of good bacteria. They help give yogurt its thickness and sour taste. Examine a bit of yogurt under a microscope and draw what you observe.

Good bacteria can even be helpful in cleaning up the environment. Some bacteria are used to eat the organic matter in sewage. The process makes sewage cleaner. Other bacteria cause garbage to decompose, or rot. A few types of bacteria can break down oil that has spilled accidentally from an oil tanker. Some other bacteria can be used to break down plastic and chemicals such as pesticides (bug killers). If oil, plastics, or pesticides are not broken down, they can be poisonous to fish, birds, plants, and other living things.

Bacteria can break down oil that has washed up on shore after an oil spill. The bacteria change the oil into substances that are less harmful to the environment and living things.

Protists

Like bacteria, **protists** (PROH-tists) are single-celled organisms. But protists are different from bacteria. They are larger, for one thing. And protists have a nucleus and other structures that bacteria do not have.

There are many varieties of protists, including protozoa (proh-tuh-ZOH-uh) and most algae. Although protists are neither plants nor animals, many protozoan protists act like animals. They can get their own food and move on their own. They can also get rid of waste products from their bodies.

Protozoan Protists

An amoeba (uh-MEE-buh) is one of the simplest protozoan protists. It is able to change its shape and can capture its food by surrounding it. The paramecium (pa-ruh-MEE-see-um) has more structures than the amoeba. It is covered with hair-like structures called cilia (SIH-lee-uh). Cilia help it move through water.

The euglena (yoo-GLEE-nuh) is a protozoan protist that acts like a plant. It contains chloroplasts and is able to make its own food. The euglena has a whip-like structure on its surface called a flagellum (fla-JEH-lum). The euglena flaps its flagellum to help it move through the water.

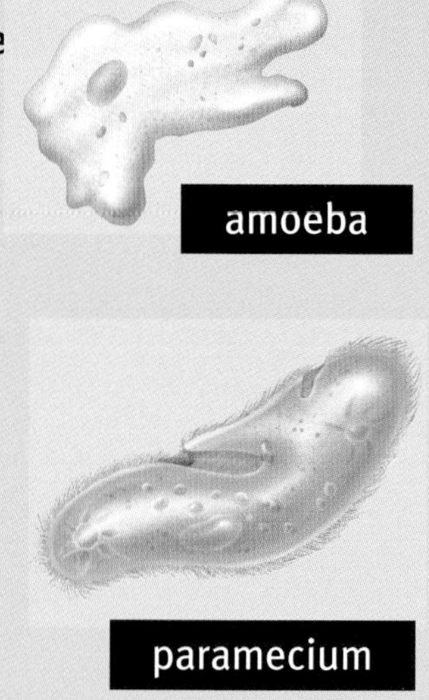

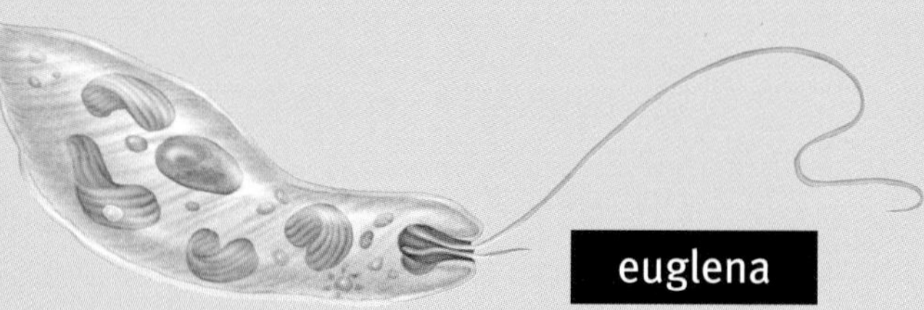

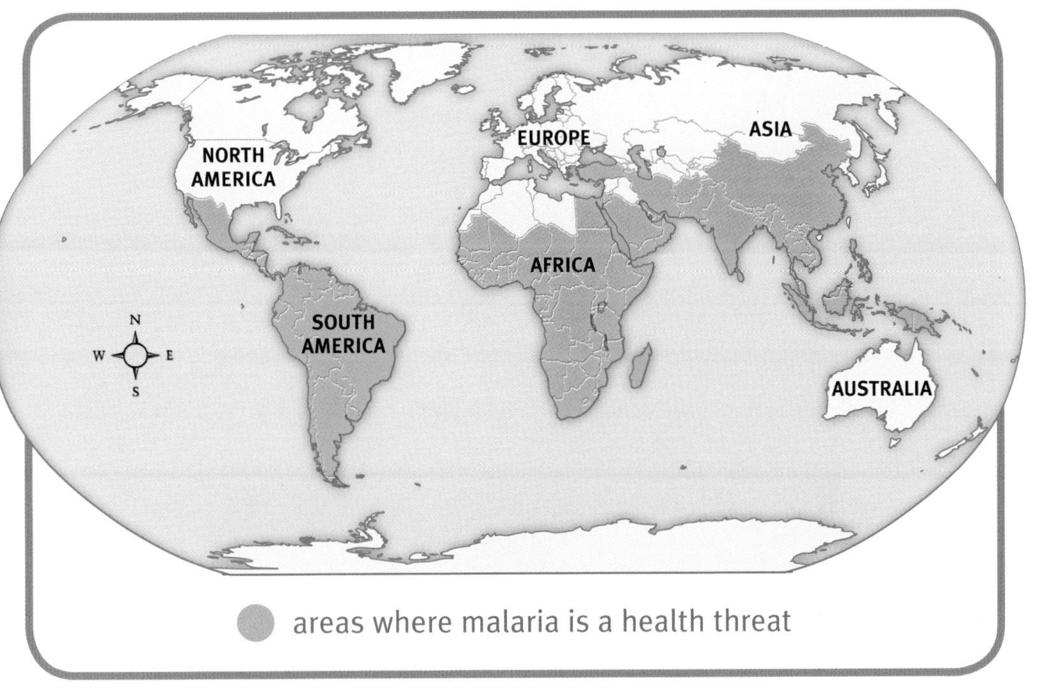

Like bacteria, some protists can cause serious diseases in humans. Malaria is a disease that features a high fever and chills. It is caused by a protozoan protist that lives in the bodies of some mosquitoes. If an infected mosquito bites a human, the malaria-causing protozoa can enter the human's body. Malaria is a serious health threat in some parts of the world.

Sleeping Sickness is another serious disease that is caused by a protozoan protist. Because the disease is found only in Africa, it is sometimes called African Sleeping Sickness. While malaria is passed to humans by a mosquito, Sleeping Sickness is transmitted to both humans and animals by a tsetse (TSEET-see) fly. Tsetse flies live on the banks of lakes and rivers in Africa.

Algae protists act like plants. Like plants, they contain chlorophyll, which makes photosynthesis happen. Some algae protists are used to make helpful products. A diatom (DY-uh-tahm) is an algae protist that has a hard shell made out of a glass-like substance. The shells of dead diatoms are ground up and added to some toothpastes and cleansers.

Other types of helpful protists are brown and red algae. These algae produce a substance that is used to thicken foods such as ice cream, gelatin, and pudding. This thickening substance is also used in some cosmetics.

So, like it or not, you might brush your teeth with, eat, or wear protists!

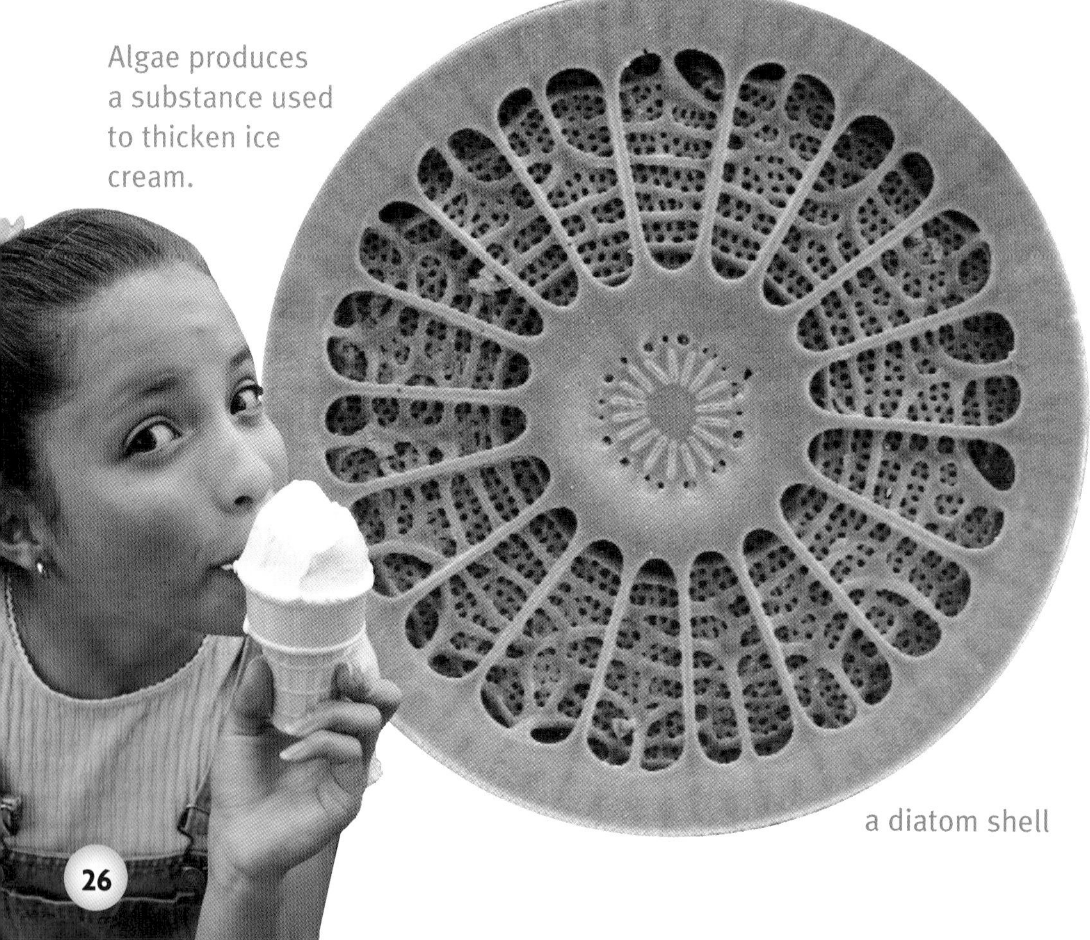

Algae produces a substance used to thicken ice cream.

a diatom shell

Viruses: Cell Invaders

A **virus** is a tiny organism that can invade living cells. Because viruses contain only certain parts of a cell, they are not considered to be living things. A virus cannot carry out any life functions unless it gets inside a living cell called a host cell.

A virus has two basic parts: a core of genetic material and an outer coat of protein that surrounds it. The core material controls the making of new virus cells. The protein coat protects the virus.

Viruses are extremely small. Scientists could not see the shapes and sizes of different viruses until the electron microscope was invented.

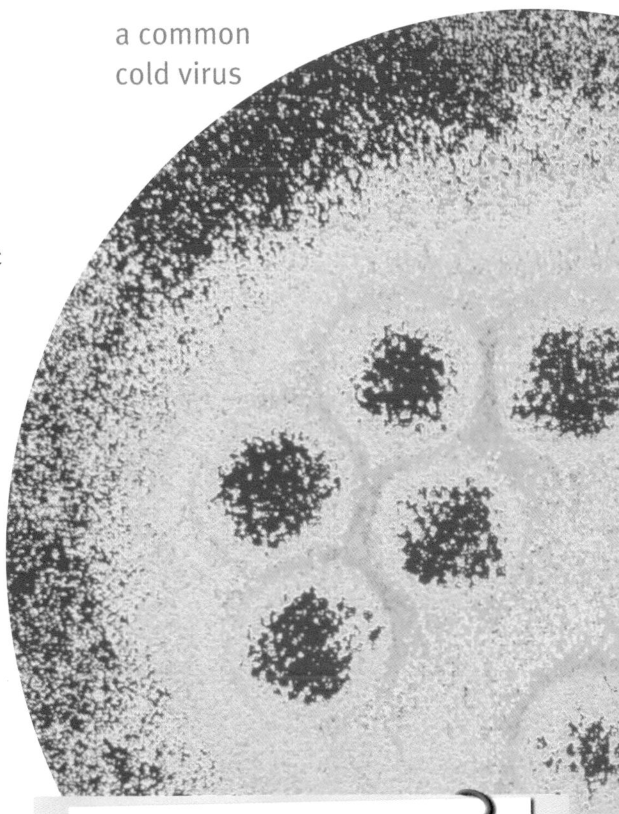

a common cold virus

SCIENCE in the News

Scientists are exploring a way to kill cancer cells using the common cold virus. Scientists weaken the virus, so it is not strong enough to affect healthy cells. They also adjust the genes in the virus to help it invade cancer cells and destroy them.

A virus uses a host cell to make new virus particles. The diagram on this page shows the four stages of a virus. First, the virus finds a host cell. Then the virus puts its genetic material into the host cell. After that, the DNA of the virus reproduces, making more viruses. Finally, the host cell bursts open and releases the new viruses. When the new viruses invade other host cells, the process begins again.

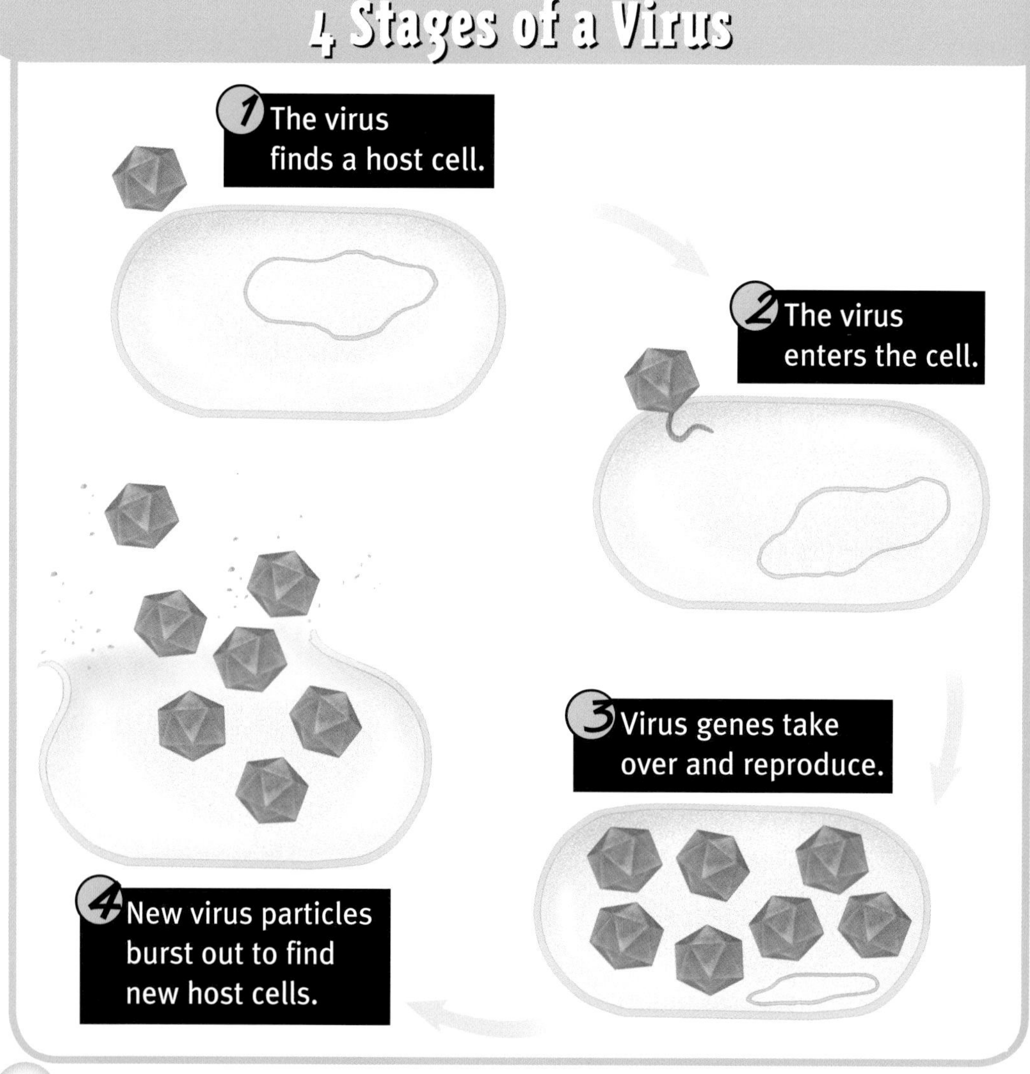

Viruses cause many diseases in humans, such as colds, flus, and measles. They also cause AIDS, smallpox, and West Nile disease. Some of these diseases can cause lasting damage to the body or even death.

Poor health can weaken our cells, and weakened cells are more vulnerable to viruses. Try to avoid getting sick by developing good habits: eat healthful foods, drink lots of water, exercise, and get a good night's sleep. It is also important to wash your hands often. Soap and water wash viruses off your hands so they are less likely to find their way into your body.

Point

Make Connections

Think back to the last time you were sick. What were the symptoms of your illness? How long were you sick? Did you have to take antibiotics or other medications to get well? Did you spread your illness to other family members or friends? Do you know whether your illness was caused by a virus, a bacteria, or a protist?

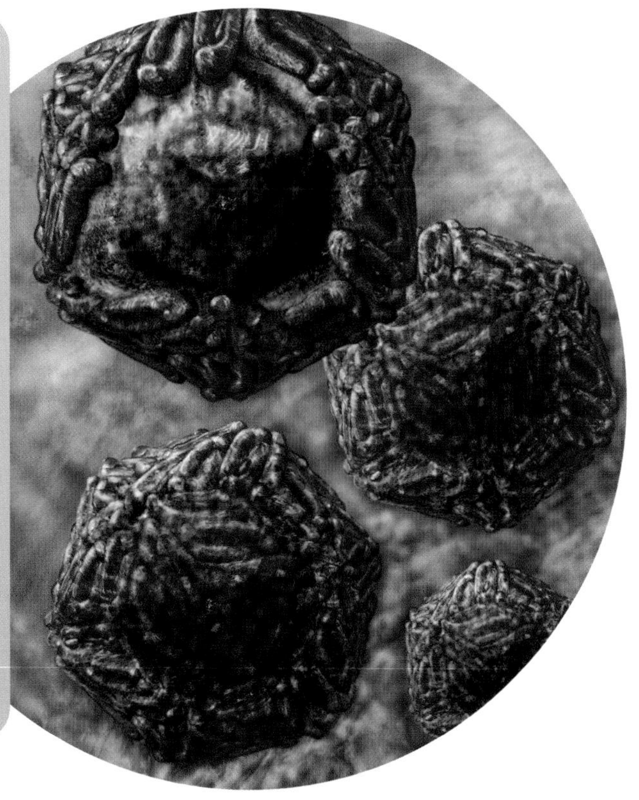

West Nile virus

Conclusion

All living things—plants and animals—are made up of cells. Each type of cell has a different size, shape, and purpose, but they all have the same three parts.

Microscopes and other types of scientific technology continue to improve. With each improvement, scientists are learning many new things about cells and the structures inside of them.

As scientists gain a better understanding of cells, they might be able to slow down, prevent, or cure certain diseases. This might allow you, your family, and your friends to live healthier, longer lives!

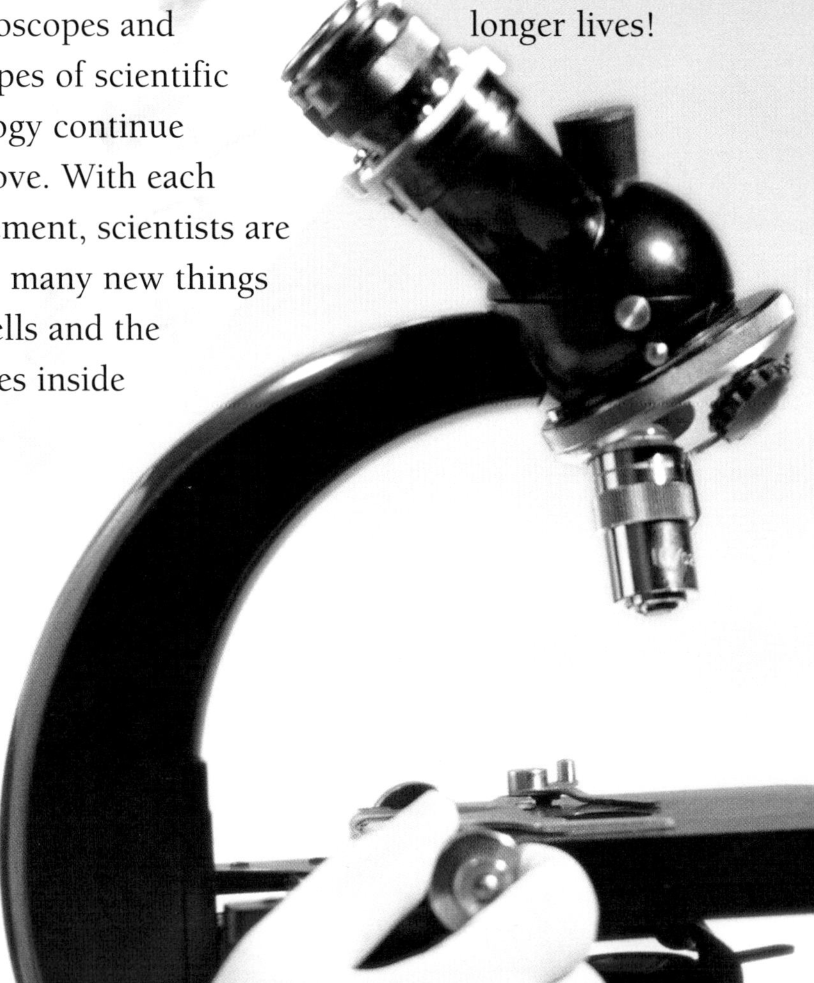

Glossary

bacteria (bak-TEER-ee-uh) single-celled organisms that do not contain a nucleus (page 5)

cell (SEL) a unit that makes up all living things (page 2)

cell membrane (SEL MEHM-brane) the thin, flexible tissue that surrounds a cell (page 12)

cell wall (SEL WAUL) the outermost boundary of plant and bacterial cells (page 17)

chloroplast (KLOR-uh-plast) a structure found in plant cells that allows plants to make their own food (page 18)

chromosome (KROH-muh-some) a long, coiled molecule made of DNA (page 14)

cytoplasm (SY-tuh-pla-zum) the material outside of a cell's nucleus (page 12)

gene (JEEN) a segment of DNA that has the instructions for building different types of cells (page 14)

nucleus (NOO-klee-us) a cell structure that contains chromosomes, which direct all the activities of the cell (page 12)

organelles (or-guh-NELZ) small structures in the cytoplasm of cells that perform different functions (page 13)

photosynthesis (foh-toh-SIN-theh-sis) the process by which plants use sunlight, water, and carbon dioxide to make their own food (page 18)

protist (PROH-tist) a single-celled organism with a nucleus (page 24)

virus (VY-rus) a tiny particle that is not living, but that can invade cells (page 27)

Index